VAPOR

Toho Publishing Chapbook Series I

Josh Martin

TOHO
PUBLISHING

Contents

Not Knocking

I've never been so small
as I was then, my breath
breaking softly against
your locked door like a wave
the sliver of light spilling
out onto the stoop where I was standing
wanting to knock but never

wanting to be heard or seen again
by anyone or you or to touch
warm skin because the cold
was numbing enough to stop me

from knocking, I just wanted to see or hear you
sitting in your kitchen
waiting for me to leave again
weeping under your breath, afraid
of the space between your body
and the door that I was so damn close to

knocking on, knowing

knowing you would let me in again
if I told you I was frozen
if I showed you I was broken
enough that if you let me go

I'd die out in the cold.

A Moment Ago

A moment ago
couldn't have been so long, could it

have been just there
where you were sitting

so far away from me but
close enough that I could tell

> *forever's almost up*
> *for us.*

Could we have really been so close
lying in that halcyon sea we disappeared to

pretending to each other

that we could actually see the stars
through the polluting light

that we weren't getting bug bites

that the dandelions around us
were actually wildflowers

worth picking and pressing and keeping
in back pockets, between pages

to be remembered and wondered at
like some enchanted fossil

Sleepy Pulse

I dislike my sober self, so
I sip you   dreamily
wincing,   exhaling
breaths like wind from flailing
tattered wings.

I touch you, but can't
get inside—
            your
                  skin
is warm but mine is losing color as
quiet constellations swim within
the dead space in your eyes
as they're spilling into mine.

You remain   circulating
whispering white noise like
my sleepy pulse singing
softly to my skeleton—
            a hollow velvet sound.

O — o

Has my darkness settled in
am I
        mixing and
eclipsing with your Blues
is my gravity hav
             ing any
   pull upon your ocean
is there something in the void between our moons?

Groan

I snapped off the arrow
that was sunk into my gut
handed you the fletching, kept
the sharpened stone and spine as
consolation.

How to Breathe

Do you ever forget how to breathe?
Misplace the rhythm
of inhales and exhales
trying to find the opportunity
between the two to speak

only to discover you
never thought of anything to say
panicking as all your most basic
biological cadences give way
to something less like living
and more like struggling to survive.

It's not like coping or letting go
but something in between
the space that's left when
we lose things

the space we used to put words in
now filled with movements
aimed away from the pain so
we don't slow down enough to feel
a thing besides our breathing

the off-pace panting
crashing through your throat, against
the back of your teeth on its way
to filling all those silent, empty spaces.

Pyre

I wonder, will
the last of what I wish for
pull away up the river in ritual
wash up smoldering against the bank
undignified and rotten

like all the other things we wanted

all those hours of ours aging in the sun
                              and almost gone
faded like the ink that tells
my story on my skin
yet impossible to change like
          the last things we said before
          it never felt the same.

I wonder, will there be weeping
as we watch it drift away
will we hear it over
          the river's heavy trickle
          the little lapping waves upon my nape
                    as though to say

that forever wasn't ever in the cards, just
the comfort of the silt in which we're sleeping.

Roaches

In the dark, my thoughts
return like roaches, their skitterings

their terrifying smallness.

Slow Dance

I was breathing deep and heavy just
so I could see my breath because
in the crisp and windless void
              it looked like you.

And in my pocket I was gripping
with frozen fingertips
a phone that like my life was either dead
or just felt that way because you weren't in it.

In my head I see monsters with my face
growling at angels, flailing with malice and
killing pretty things
          just to sob off in the darkness once
the sun shows up again
to shed light on what's savage
about me

what's fucking brutal
about the weakness of my spirit

but when the strings begin to hum
I still scan the room for you

reach out my hand for
a slow dance, the only
dance you can do sadly
but with love.

Night Sweats

I anticipate exhaling blades
of an oscillating fan
waiting in want for each
cool blue brush stroke over
my bare feet, shedding my
blanket like charred flesh floating
in an oil rig explosion
my damp and burning soles below me
as I shiver and chatter
my teeth, that harrowing sound
my dentist thinks I'm making in my sleep
the soreness of my eyes
as I peek to the side, bouncing between
my cell phone and the window and
I start to smell the sun
as the glass begins to glow.

Blue Light

With a sigh I fogged the pane
I sat beside, obscuring
an image of the world with rested breath
sinking, comfortably tracing
with sleepy eyes a trail of clarity left
by the sweat bead sliding
down the icy glass between me and

a birdless sky—
a sun that doesn't stay

crumbling roads and walkways
relatably unwarmed and in decay
the rattlings of twigs like little bones
dragged across the sidewalk by the wind
convincing me to stay frozen
          inside, hovered over

the false heat of a blue light I'm holding in my hand.

Empty After

I sat at the edge of the bed
my back to some fiery thing I followed
like a star that it would save my life to hold

but when I was close enough to touch it
I approached so fucking softly
it couldn't even tell I was inside and

for a moment there it even lost its shine
because of me.

At a shameful pace I slip into my clothing
that doesn't fit as well now that I'm shrinking
shriveling in the presence
of yet another star
swallowing its light inside my void

outed again for my illness

my joyless, bloodless body making
a joke out of my ache for love again.

It gets worse with each encounter
the darkness more consuming
more part of me now than the light was before

so much so that at night I don't
look up anymore
don't show my face to something that might want me

afraid that if it's bright enough
someone else will see my withered form.

Overcast

You came to me
misted eyes

unglowing under the overcast
your mouth rested open hoping
for a sip of closeness
to me

as though I'd be warm
enough to boost your color
when at best I could accentuate your grays

unearth a muted blue or two between
dozens of disappointments
you've grown accustomed to

because of me, my
passionless companionship you've yet
to replace with better memories.

Instead you're soaking from the rain
you trudged through on your way back into town
and past your shriveled frame
I start to sense it rolling in

the familiar stormy scent pursuing you
the fog we used to scare away
by fucking and fighting loudly

and it's impossible not to feel
like I'm responsible

and it hurts
that it was I who learned this first, but

you can't kill the void with something liquid
can't drown out the empty
by swallowing the rain.

Imperfect Blue

A fog of familiar sounds
spills my way from the homestead
       tumbling between peaks
whispering sweetly

absolutely nothing to me.

I'm dry to the bone
but reek of rainwater

mumbling little tunes to
myself about the moon

shriveling at the wrists while
conducting a quiet choir, listening
for hypnotic knocks of water drop-
           lets oozing past
the blue stained glass and I
have something to be missing.

I   ache
for saturation.

I rest with my shadow
coiling my neck
surrendering my eyes to sleep
each night
over
again.

Watercolor Eye

In the shallows of my skin I feel
my turbid blood malnourish me

polluting with impunity un-
til it turns violent, violet

showing through my face
like a patient it's too late for

a dawdling bruise
or something I should have said

but didn't—and now I can't
since the salt I lost in night sweats

has left me bland and flavorless
sketching expressions of myself

I often fail to recognize
portraits and stories that escape me

forever, seducing you like inky plumes
I've sputtered in a panic, imprecisely

consumed, discarded, left out to decay
shivering and shaky like palms collecting rain.

Petrichor

A pacifying breeze
seeps in through the patio screen
at the speed
    of smoke
during a summer dusk as the distance
wraps itself up—sleepily
in a vapor blanket
rumbles lowly, spills out
over olive painted hills on its way into
the room I sit dryly inside of—shielded from its
weeping
emptying myself, releasing
the musty ruminations of the day
dissipating into plumes of vacant static
collapsing the bony scaffolding inside me
        to make space in my lungs
for that sweet, stony liquid
as I quietly pass away at will
the lie that I feel
so bad.

Stone

What's left of me
after the erosion
is reduced to something smooth
something to be skipped across the creek

by a boy just like me, his father
reminding him that it's

        all in the wrist

slung across the surface as
        the envy of the sediment
alive and leaving ripples in its wake

reverberating circles

like paintings of the sound
that crispy
        quickening staccato that you follow
        with an ever-growing grin, ever-
            lifting your cheeks and eyelids until

it's settled in the bank across the creek
at someone else's feet
and even smoother.

Indian Beach—September 7

T'was fuckin perfect weather
the day I found my favorite place on the planet
back behind that bulging
coal-faced boulder in the shallows

a solitary rock—the shape of a turtle

covered with a mix of moss and shelly jungle
sharp to the touch but wasn't shit
against a wet suit.

I arrived in unguided style
windburnt from the journey west
in search of something evergreen
a painless place where it wouldn't matter

how long it took to get there
who fell off along the way
          whose fault it was or
if any of it even had to happen.

So I sat upon a stone
tired bones pulsing with the Pacific

tickled by Poseidon's dainty whims
                    I grinned

I waved myself goodbye, for a time
siphoned in some wind and
      salt to scrape me clean
and
I was never that alone again.

Parts

Everywhere our pieces lie around
out of context
each one of me, maybe
or you or something
wholly unrelated
for strangers to behold

to appreciate because
they see themselves
in our discolored skin
the wet, aching muscle and
the fractured skeletons
we all seem to share with one another.

The truth is that when we break
no matter where we are
what pieces we pick up
to take with us
it's the parts we put together
that make us
that define us on our way
to finally making sense
of something.

When we break, we misplace
a spattering of fragments
too tiny or
too heavy to pick up
all those parts a part
of *absolutely nothing*
anymore

until they're found by someone else
buried under leaves
in the pockets of jeans, between
cushions on couches
once-missing pieces to be seen
and discovered as a whole
separate something.

Acknowledgments

Thank you to the people and the communities who made the creation of this chapbook possible.

To my family, for being a constant reminder of how much I have to be thankful for. To my tribe—the writers and poets of Green Street Poetry—for your contagious enthusiasm for honing your craft. To Andrés Cruciani for always pushing me to the next level and for creating a platform through which this story can be told. To my editor, instructor, and friend Sean Hanrahan for chiseling away at this collection until it was ready. And to the other students of the Toho Publishing Chapbook Course, whose reviews, encouragement, and suggestions helped this book find its voice.

I also want to thank the creators whose art, writing, and music helped inspire and influence the work in this chapbook: Sam Fischer, Emily Conlon, Justin Vernon, and Ali John Meredith-Lacey.

And most importantly, I want to thank my fiancée, Nikki Whitney, for making me better and brave enough to create this, for filling my life with light, and for building beautiful things with me—always. I love you more than you could know.

About the Poet

Josh Martin is a poet, entrepreneur, and professional marketer based in Philadelphia. He is the founder of Green Street Poetry, an organization that provides free poetry workshops, readings, and open mics in his community. His poetry has most recently been featured in *Toho Journal*, the *Philadelphia Secret Admirer*, and the Italian-American literary journal *Ovunque Siamo*.

When he isn't writing, Josh keeps busy providing marketing services for non-profits and professional service firms around Philadelphia, hanging with his cats Jonah and Harper, or drinking wine on weeknights with his fiancée, Nicole.

Made in the USA
Middletown, DE
20 February 2021